A Robbie Reader

Where Did All the Dinosaurs Go?

Russell Roberts

P.O. Box 196
Hockessin, Delaware 19707
Visit us on the web: www.mitchelllane.com
Comments?email us:
mitchelllane@mitchelllane.com

Printing   1   2   3   4   5   6   7   8   9

A Robbie Reader/Natural Disasters
Earthquake in Loma Prieta, California, 1989
The Fury of Hurricane Andrew, 1992
Mt. Vesuvius and the Destruction of Pompeii, A.D. 79
Mudslide in La Conchita, California, 2005
Tsunami Disaster in Indonesia, 2004
Where Did All the Dinosaurs Go?

Library of Congress Cataloging-in-Publication Data
Roberts, Russell.
    Where did all the dinosaurs go? / by Russell Roberts.
        p. cm. — (Natural Disasters — what can we learn?)
    Includes bibliographical references and index.
    ISBN 1-58415-420-9 (library bound)
    1. Dinosaurs — Extinction — Juvenile literature. 2. Reptiles, Fossil — Juvenile literature.
I. Title. II. Series.
QE861.6.E95R63 2005
567.9 — dc22
                                                                              2005009691

ABOUT THE AUTHOR: Russell Roberts has written and published over 35 books for adults and children on a variety of subjects, including baseball, memory power, business, New Jersey history, and travel. He has also written numerous books for Mitchell Lane, such as *Pedro Menendez de Aviles, Philo Farnsworth Invents TV, Robert Goddard, Bernardo de Galvez,* and *Mt. Vesuvius and the Destruction of Pompeii, A.D. 79*. He lives in Bordentown, New Jersey, with his family and a fat, fuzzy, and crafty calico cat named Rusti.

PHOTO CREDITS: Cover composite by Jamie Kondrchek; title page — M. Kulyk/ Photo Researchers; p. 4 — Jacana/Photo Researchers; p. 6 — Stephen J. Krasemann/Photo Researchers; pp. 7, 9, 16 — Roger Harris/Photo Researchers; p. 10 — Francois Gohier/ Photo Researchers; pp. 12, 15 — Chase Studio/Photo Researchers; p. 13 — Sheila Terry/ Photo Researchers; p. 14 — Chris Butler/Photo Researchers; p. 19 — G. I. Bernard/Photo Researchers; p. 20 — Sherwin Crasto/AP Wide World; p. 24 — D. van Ravenswaay/ Photo Researchers; p. 26 — John R. Foster/Photo Researchers; p. 27 — C. Butler/Photo Researchers; p. 28 — Mark Garlick/Photo Researchers.

TABLE OF CONTENTS

Words in **bold** type can be found in the glossary.

Diplodocus (dih-PLAH-duh-cus) was a plant-eating dinosaur.

A DIFFERENT WORLD

Picture the world millions of years ago. A large dinosaur is standing in a lake. It is eating a plant. The earth's **climate** (KLY-met) is different than it is today. It is warmer. There are lots of plants that grow well in warm weather.

Large creatures are swimming in the oceans. Some fly in the air. Smaller animals scurry about on the ground. But mainly there are dinosaurs of all sizes. Some peacefully eat plants. Others are meat eaters. Meat eaters eat other animals—including dinosaurs!

There are no people there. Most of the animals that you can name today do not exist, either. Dinosaurs rule the world.

Ornithomimus (or-NIH-thoe-MIE-mus), or "bird mimic," was like an ostrich in some ways. It could run faster than 35 miles per hour.

The dinosaur in the lake keeps eating. It probably does not think about the future. It does not think that someday all the dinosaurs might be gone.

But they will.

This flying reptile, called a pteranodon (teh-RAH-nuh-don), lived about 80 million years ago. It ate a lot of fish.

7

What happened to the dinosaurs?

That is a question people have been asking for many years. It is a big mystery. No one knows the answer.

Dinosaurs lived on the earth for over 180 million years. You have probably heard of them. Maybe you have seen drawings of them in books. Perhaps you have seen them in movies or on television.

One dinosaur was *Tyrannosaurus* (tie-RAN-oh-SAWR-us) *rex*. Sometimes it is called T. rex. It was 20 feet tall. Its teeth were sharp as knives. It had two small front arms and walked on its strong back legs. T. rex was a meat eater. Movies often use T. rex when they want to show a scary dinosaur.

Not all dinosaurs were so frightening. *Brachiosaurus* (bray-kee-o-SAWR-us) was one of the largest dinosaurs. It was as long as two school buses put end to end. It ate plants and was peaceful. *Apatosaurus* (uh-POT-uh-SAWR-us) was another large dinosaur. It could be 90 feet long and also ate plants.

These are just three of the many kinds of dinosaurs. But why are they not here anymore?

Tyrannosaurus rex was a meat-eating dinosaur.

These scientists are digging dinosaur bones out of the ground.

DIGGING FOR DINOSAURS

One day in 1838, a farmer in New Jersey was digging a hole. He found a very large black bone. It was too big to belong to any animal he knew.

Over the years the farmer sometimes found more big bones. His neighbors heard about them. They came to look at them. What could they be? What animal could they have come from? No one knew. The farmer gave away pieces of the big bones as gifts.

This went on for 20 years. Then a scientist named Joseph Leidy heard about the bones. He came to look at them. He got very excited. He thought they could be dinosaur bones.

Bones from *Hadrosaurus* were first found in New Jersey. *Hadrosaurus* may have looked like the dinosaurs drawn above.

They were. Leidy dug up many more bones. He took them to a **museum** (mew-ZEE-um). When they were put together, the bones formed a complete dinosaur skeleton. It was the first complete skeleton to be found in the United States. It was called *Hadrosaurus* (had-ruh-SAWR-us).

People have not always known about dinosaurs. The word *dinosaur* did not exist until 1842, when an English scientist named Richard Owen invented it. He combined two Greek words that mean "terrible lizard." He said his new word described creatures that had once lived on the earth.

Since the early 1800s, scientists have found dinosaur bones all over the world. Sometimes they even find dinosaur eggs. Their discoveries help them form **theories** (THEER-eez). Theories are explanations. Theories try to answer questions.

Richard Owen was one of the first dinosaur scientists. He invented the word *dinosaur*.

13

Scientists have found fossil clues that some dinosaurs may have had feathers.

For example, some scientists question how dinosaurs could be related to birds. Some dinosaurs had hipbones that are similar to birds' hipbones. Fossil prints of feathers have been found near dinosaur bones. Using the evidence of hipbones, feathers, and eggs, these scientists formed a theory. They think that birds **evolved** (ee-VOL-vd) from dinosaurs. They believe that birds are modern dinosaurs. Other scientists disagree.

Dromaeosaurus (droe-MAE-yoe-SAWR-us) had bird-like traits. The artist who drew this picture imagined it also had a plume of feathers on its head.

There is still much more about dinosaurs to learn. Scientists find new information all the time. There are many more types of dinosaurs to discover. There are many more theories to test. And there is one question that still puzzles them all: What happened to the dinosaurs?

The horns on this triceratops (tri-SAYR-ah-tops) were used to fight other dinosaurs. The triceratops lived in North America about 67 million years ago.

EXTINCTION

When a **species** (SPEE-sheez) of plant or animal dies out, it becomes **extinct** (EX-tinkt). It no longer exists. That is what happened to the dinosaurs about 65 million years ago.

Many species have become extinct. One **estimate** (ES-tih-met) is that 99 percent of all species that ever lived are extinct. There have been five different times, all long ago, when many species became extinct at once. These are called periods of great death.

When the dinosaurs died out, they were not the only species to go extinct. About 70 percent of all species at that time also disappeared. That means 7 out of every 10

species died. It is the most famous period of great death in history.

But some species did not die. Thirty percent lived. That means 3 out of every 10 species lived. Crocodiles and frogs are two species that survived. They are still alive today. But the dinosaurs did not live, and scientists do not know why.

Sometimes we know why a species becomes extinct. Once there was a very common bird in the United States called a passenger pigeon. So many flew together that they were like black clouds. In the 1850s, people hunted them for food. They never thought that they could hunt the pigeons until they became extinct. But they did. The last one died in a zoo in 1914. No one will ever see a passenger pigeon again.

Have you ever seen a heath hen? How about a great auk or a Stellar's sea cow? These are other animals you will never see. They became extinct within the last few hundred years. People caused them to become extinct.

But there were no people on the earth when dinosaurs became extinct. People could not have caused them to disappear.

People hunted the passenger pigeon for food. It became extinct in 1914.

Dr. Vikas Amte, a scientist, is examining dinosaur eggs. The eggs were found by farmers in India.

REJECTED THEORIES

There have been many theories about what happened to the dinosaurs. Theories try to explain how facts fit together. Remember that theories are just possible reasons. When scientists formed these theories, the theories seemed right. But now some of them seem wrong.

One theory looks at when new plants appeared. It explains that the new plants had flowers. The dinosaurs were not used to these plants. The plants made them sick, and the dinosaurs died.

Scientists feel that this theory is not right. Many flowering plants died at the same time as the dinosaurs. Recall that 7 out of 10 species

on earth died. How could flowering plants kill the dinosaurs if the plants also died?

Another theory says that dinosaurs gave germs to each other. These germs caused diseases that killed them.

Scientists have found no evidence of a dinosaur disease, so this theory probably is not right either.

There is a theory that dinosaurs got too big. Being so big was not healthy. They could not live normally. This big size killed them.

This is like the germ theory. There is no evidence to support it, so scientists feel this theory is wrong too.

Another theory says mammals caused the dinosaurs to die. Mammals are animals that have fur. Their babies drink their mother's milk. The babies of almost all mammals are born live. They do not hatch from eggs. People, dogs, and cats are mammals. A dinosaur is not a mammal. Its babies hatched from eggs.

Large mammals began appearing on the earth around the time the dinosaurs died. Some scientists have said that these mammals ate dinosaur eggs. The mammals ate the eggs faster than the dinosaurs could lay them. Finally there were no more dinosaur babies, so dinosaurs died out.

Mammals may have eaten dinosaur eggs, but they could not have eaten all the eggs. They would have run out of food if they had. They too would have become extinct. Scientists have figured that this is another theory that seems wrong.

There is a theory that says something happened in outer space. Maybe a star exploded. This caused deadly rays to hit the earth. These rays were similar to sunlight but much more harmful. The rays killed the dinosaurs. But scientists have never found any evidence of these harmful rays in the dinosaur bones they have dug up.

These are just some theories that seem incorrect. What about some that may be right?

As this painting suggests, if an asteroid or comet struck the earth, the blast would have scorched the land and plants and beasts. Smoke and dust would have blocked the sun and poisoned the air. Many species would not have survived.

POSSIBLE THEORIES

What killed the dinosaurs? Many scientists blame a climate change. They think the climate became cooler. Dinosaurs could not adjust to cooler weather, and they died.

Scientists feel climate change may also explain why so many other species died, both land and sea creatures. But what kind of natural disaster could have caused the climate to change?

Some scientists think that something on the earth happened to change the climate. Maybe volcanoes (vahl-KAY-nose) erupted. Dust and dirt could have been thrown into the air. The dust and dirt made giant dark clouds that blocked the sun. The earth got cooler.

This painting shows how an asteroid may have looked as it struck the earth.

Clouds of dust blocking sunlight is not unusual. In 1815 a volcano named Tambora erupted. It put so much dust and dirt into the air that the weather changed. It rained a lot in some places. In other places it did not rain at all. The summer was cold. In the United States, 1816 was called the "year without a summer."

Other scientists have a different idea. They believe that a giant **asteroid** (AS-tur-oyd) struck the earth. It caused huge fires and floods. It also caused a big dust cloud. The dust cloud changed the weather. This killed many dinosaurs.

Scientists have found evidence for both the volcano and the asteroid theory. But there is not enough evidence to prove either one.

Other scientists reject the climate theories. Some of them think that a group of

The asteroid would have made such a loud sound when it hit that even dinosaurs far away may have noticed it.

Did comets in the sky signal the approach of an asteroid?

comets (KAH-mets) caused the extinctions on the earth. Comets travel far out into space, then swing back close to the sun again. Scientists say one large group of comets comes every 26 million years. Every time they come, many species die.

What is right? What is wrong? No one knows. The search for answers continues.

Maybe one day you will be a scientist. Maybe you will be the one who solves the mystery: Why did dinosaurs become extinct?

TIMELINE

Tertiary Period
65–2 million years ago (mya)
Earliest large mammals   65 mya*

Cretaceous-Tertiary Boundary
65 million years ago
Extinction of the dinosaurs

Cretaceous Period
144–65 million years ago
    Triceratops   67–65 mya
    Tyrannosaurus rex   67–65 mya
    Ornithomimus   70 mya
    Parasaurolophus (a hadrosaur)   76–65 mya
    Dromaeosaurus   76–74 mya
    Pteranodon   85–75 mya
    Velociraptor   84–80 mya

Jurassic Period
208–144 million years ago
    Archaeopteryx   150 mya
    Brachiosaurus   155–140 mya
    Diplodocus   155–145 mya
    Apatosaurus   154–145 mya

Triassic Period
248–208 million years ago
Earliest dinosaurs

*Million years ago

FIND OUT MORE

Books

Asimov, Isaac, and Richard Hantula. *What Killed the Dinosaurs?* Milwaukee, Wisconsin: Gareth Stevens, 2004.

Berger, Melvin, and Gloria Berger. *Why Did the Dinosaurs Disappear? The Great Dinosaur Mystery.* Nashville, Tennessee: Ideals Publications, 1995.

Coleman, Graham. *Countdown to Dinosaur Doom!* Hauppauge, New York: Barron's Educational Series, 1995.

Dodson, Peter. *An Alphabet of Dinosaurs.* New York: Scholastic, 1995.

Jacobs, Marian. *Why Did the Dinosaurs Become Extinct?* New York: PowerKids Press, 1999.

Nardo, Don. *The Extinction of the Dinosaurs.* San Diego: KidHaven Press, 2004.

Oxlade, Chris. *The Mystery of the Death of the Dinosaurs.* Chicago: Heinemann Library, 2002.

Wood, A. J. *Countdown to Extinction: A Hologram Adventure to Prehistoric Times.* New York: Disney Press, 1998.

On the Internet

Dinosaur Extinction—Enchanted Learning
http://www.enchantedlearning.com/subjects/dinosaurs/extinction/Asteroid.html

Mesozoic Dinosaurs–Enchanted Learning
http://www.enchantedlearning.com/subjects/
    dinosaurs/mesozoic/
Dinosaur Floor
http://www.cotf.edu/ete/modules/msese/
    dinosaur.html

GLOSSARY

asteroid (AS-tur-oyd)–a rocky object in outer space found mostly between Mars and Jupiter.

climate (KLY-met)–a combination of temperature, wind, and rain.

comets (KAH-mets)–objects in outer space with a body that is mostly ice and dust and, when they orbit close to the sun, a long, glowing tail.

estimate (ES-teh-met)–a thoughtful guess.

evolved (ee-VOLVD)–grew and changed.

extinct (ex-TINKT)–no longer exists.

museum (mew-ZEE-um)–a place where objects of value are kept and displayed.

species (SPEE-sheez)–a group of living things with many features in common.

INDEX